The Textbook on Role of Prakriti in Ayurgenomics and Genomics in Modern Healthcare Systems

Dr. Supriya Tonge

Associate Professor [M.D., Ph.D Scholar]

Dr. Gaurav Gairola [M.D.]

Assistant Professor

Dr. Sujit Kumar [M.D.]

Assistant Professor

Title   : The Textbook on Role of Prakriti in Ayurgenomics
                  and Genomics in Modern Healthcare Systems

Author   : Dr. Supriya Tonge, Dr. Gaurav Gairola, Dr. Sujit Kumar

Edition   : First (December, 2024)

ISBN   : 9788197950506

Published by

Regd. Add.: 254, Khuriyakhatta No. 10, Bindukhatta,
Lalkuan, Nainital - 262402, Uttarakhand, India
Website : www.prachidigital.com
E-mail : info@prachidigital.in
Phone : +91 976041 7980, +91 976041 8103

Printed by :
Manipal Technologies Limited, Bengaluru - 560001, Karnataka

Preface

The intricate interplay between traditional wisdom and modern scientific advancements has paved the way for innovative approaches to healthcare. The concept of *Prakriti*, deeply rooted in *Ayurveda*, offers a unique perspective on individualized medicine by emphasizing the innate constitution of an individual. *Ayurgenomics*, an emerging field that bridges *Ayurveda* and genomics, is redefining how we perceive health, disease, and therapeutic strategies in the modern healthcare system.

This work delves into the profound role of *Prakriti* in *Ayurgenomics* and its implications for genomics in contemporary healthcare. By integrating the *Ayurvedic* principle of individualized constitution with genomic science, this interdisciplinary field seeks to establish a personalized approach to disease prevention, diagnosis, and treatment. The ability to correlate *Prakriti* with genomic variations and metabolic profiles has immense potential to revolutionize our understanding of precision medicine.

This book provides an in-depth exploration of the theoretical and practical aspects of *Prakriti* and its scientific validation in *Ayurgenomics*. The initial chapters present a detailed review of the classical *Ayurvedic* concept of *Prakriti*, its classification, and its relevance in determining predispositions to various diseases. Subsequent sections highlight the integration of genomic technologies in decoding the genetic basis of *Prakriti* and its applications in identifying biomarkers for diseases, drug metabolism, and therapeutic efficacy.

Furthermore, the book emphasizes the transformative role of *Ayurgenomics* in bridging traditional healthcare systems with modern medicine, showcasing its applications in clinical settings. It also discusses the challenges and prospects of incorporating *Ayurveda* into mainstream healthcare, underscoring the need for interdisciplinary collaborations to validate and expand this promising field.

The insights presented in this book aim to foster a deeper understanding of how ancient wisdom can complement modern scientific methodologies. It is intended for researchers, clinicians, students, and anyone interested in the confluence of *Ayurveda*, genomics, and personalized medicine.

We hope this work inspires further exploration and innovation in the field of *Ayurgenomics*, contributing to a holistic and integrated approach to healthcare.

With this endeavor, we aim to not only honor the rich legacy of *Ayurveda* but also to demonstrate its relevance and adaptability in addressing the complexities of modern health challenges.

Foreword

The integration of ancient wisdom with cutting-edge scientific advancements marks a pivotal moment in the evolution of healthcare. *Ayurveda*, with its millennia-old understanding of individuality and health, offers profound insights into personalized medicine through the concept of *Prakriti*. This constitution-based approach emphasizes the unique biological and psychological composition of everyone, underscoring the importance of tailored healthcare interventions.

In recent years, the burgeoning field of *Ayurgenomics* has demonstrated how *Prakriti* can be scientifically explored and validated using genomic technologies. By aligning *Ayurveda's* time-tested principles with genomics, we are beginning to uncover genetic underpinnings that not only define an individual's *Prakriti* but also influence their susceptibility to diseases, response to therapies, and overall health outcomes. This convergence has the potential to transform the way we understand and implement personalized medicine.

The work presented in this book, "Role of *Prakriti* in *Ayurgenomics* and Genomics in the Modern Healthcare System," is a pioneering effort to elucidate the relevance of *Ayurveda* in the context of genomics and its application in contemporary healthcare. It offers an extensive exploration of *Prakriti*, its scientific validation, and its implications for precision medicine. The book bridges the gap between the traditional and the modern, providing a roadmap for integrating *Ayurveda* with genomic science to address current and future health challenges.

Through detailed discussions, the author highlights the immense potential of *Ayurgenomics* in identifying genetic markers for disease prediction, drug metabolism, and therapeutic efficacy. Moreover, this work emphasizes the role of *Prakriti*-based approaches in preventive healthcare, offering insights into how personalized interventions can promote health and longevity.

The significance of this book lies in its ability to inspire a paradigm shift. It not only enriches our understanding of personalized medicine but also reinforces the importance of interdisciplinary collaboration in advancing global health. The synergy between *Ayurveda* and genomics, as demonstrated here, is a testament to the enduring relevance of traditional knowledge in addressing modern healthcare needs.

I commend Dr. Sujit Kumar for this remarkable contribution to the field of *Ayurgenomics*. His in-depth exploration and innovative perspectives will undoubtedly serve as a valuable resource for clinicians, researchers, students, and policymakers alike. This book is a testament to the endless possibilities that arise when we integrate the wisdom of the past with the technologies of the future.

It is my honor and privilege to introduce this important work, which I am confident will inspire and guide future endeavors in the realm of personalized medicine and holistic healthcare.

PRINCIPAL

VIVEK COLLEGE OF AYURVEDIC SCIENCES AND HOSPITAL

BIJNOR, UTTAR PRADESH

Foreword

The convergence of traditional *Ayurveda* and modern genomics has opened new avenues for personalized healthcare. In this rapidly evolving field, the concept of *Prakriti*—a cornerstone of *Ayurvedic* philosophy—has gained significant attention for its potential role in guiding individualized therapeutic approaches.

By integrating *Prakriti* with genomics, *Ayurgenomics* seeks to uncover genetic markers that align with the classical *Ayurvedic* understanding of health and disease predisposition. This synergy holds immense promise for transforming the modern healthcare system.

It is with great pride and privilege that I write this foreword for Dr. Supriya Tonge's work on the "Role of *Prakriti* in *Ayurgenomics* and Genomics in the Modern Healthcare System." This scholarly endeavor offers a profound exploration of how *Prakriti*—rooted in *Ayurvedic* tradition—can inform the emerging field of genomics, paving the way for advancements in precision medicine.

Dr. Supriya Tonge's meticulous research delves into the theoretical foundation of *Prakriti*, its classification, and its relevance in understanding individual variations in health, disease susceptibility, and therapeutic responses. The book highlights the integration of *Ayurvedic* principles with state-of-the-art genomic tools, providing evidence for the relevance of *Prakriti* in modern healthcare.

Through detailed analysis and examples, it underscores how *Ayurgenomics* can help identify biomarkers for disease prediction, optimize therapeutic strategies, and promote preventive healthcare. The significance of this work lies in its ability to bridge the gap between traditional and contemporary systems of medicine.

Dr. Supriya Tonge's approach not only validates the scientific basis of *Ayurveda* but also demonstrates its applicability in addressing global health challenges. This book serves as a valuable resource for researchers, clinicians, and students, fostering interdisciplinary dialogue and innovation in the field of personalized medicine.

As the Head of the Department of Kriya Sharir at Vivek college of Ayurvedic Sciences and Hospital, Bijnor, Uttar Pradesh, it brings me great satisfaction to witness such pioneering contributions to the field. Dr. Supriya Tonge's work is a testament to the enduring relevance of *Ayurveda* and its potential to complement modern medical science.

I am confident that this book will inspire further research and innovation in *Ayurgenomics*, setting a benchmark for future studies in the field. It is a commendable effort that reflects both academic rigor and a deep commitment to advancing healthcare.

I extend my heartfelt congratulations to Dr. Supriya Tonge for this remarkable achievement and wish her continued success in her academic and professional journey.

Dr. Mangal

H.O.D. and Professor,

Department of Kriya Sharir

Institute of Ayurvedic Studies and Research

Shri Krishna AYUSH Govt. Ayurvedic Medical College

Kurukshetra, Haryana

Table of Contents

Chapter 1

Introduction to Prakriti

1.1 Definition and Concept

Prakriti, a fundamental concept in Ayurveda, refers to the inherent constitution or natural state of an individual. The term "Prakriti" is derived from the Sanskrit root words "Pra" (before) and "Kriti" (creation or doing), signifying the natural state of creation or the inherent constitution established at the time of conception.

1.2 Historical Background

Prakriti has been elaborated in classical Ayurvedic texts such as Charaka Samhita, Sushruta Samhita, and Ashtanga Hridaya. Ancient sages recognized the importance of individualized medicine and emphasized the role of Prakriti in determining the health and disease patterns of individuals.

Charaka Samhita

प्रकृतिस्त्रिविधा प्रोक्ता दोषाणां सम्प्रवृत्तये। विकृतिः सप्तधा प्रोक्ता दोषाणां विकृतेः क्रमात्॥

(चरक संहिता, सूत्र स्थान, अध्याय 7, श्लोक 39)

"Prakriti is classified into three types for the initiation of doshas, while Vikriti is classified into seven types for the disorder of doshas."

Sushruta Samhita

प्रकृतिरेव चोक्ता सा दोषाणां प्रकृतिर्गुणाः। सर्वेषां च शरीराणां प्रकृतिश्चेति मे मतम्॥

(सुश्रुत संहिता, सूत्र स्थान, अध्याय 15, श्लोक 41)

"Prakriti is described as the inherent nature of doshas, which is the natural constitution of all bodies."

Chapter 2

Vyutpatti and Nirukti of Prakriti

2.1 Etymology (Vyutpatti)

The term "Prakriti" is derived from the Sanskrit roots "Pra" (before) and "Kriti" (creation or doing). It signifies the natural state of creation or the inherent constitution established at the time of conception.

2.2 (Nirukti)

Prakriti can be interpreted as the fundamental nature or inherent qualities that determine an individual's physical, mental, and emotional attributes. It encompasses the unique combination of the three doshas (Vata, Pitta, and Kapha) that manifest at the time of conception and remain constant throughout life.

Chapter 3

Various Definitions and Synonyms of Prakriti

3.1 Definitions in Classical Texts

Charaka Samhita

दोषाः प्रकृतिवैषम्यमृषिभिश्च प्रकीर्तिताः। प्रकृत्या तु तथायुक्तं विकारमिति मे मतम्॥

(चरक संहिता, सूत्र स्थान, अध्याय 7, श्लोक 41)

"The imbalance of doshas is termed as Vikriti, while their natural balance is referred to as Prakriti."

Sushruta Samhita

प्रकृतिरेव च दोषाणां प्रकृतिर्गुणशब्दिता। सर्वेषां च शरीराणां प्रकृतिश्चेति निश्चितम्॥

(सुश्रुत संहिता, सूत्र स्थान, अध्याय 15, श्लोक 43)

"Prakriti is the inherent nature of doshas, which is considered as the natural constitution of all bodies."

Ashtanga Hridaya

प्रकृतिः प्रकृतिस्थानां दोषाणां योगमेव च। तदा तु विकृतिः प्रोक्ता यदा दोषास्तथा गताः॥

(अष्टांग हृदय, सूत्र स्थान, अध्याय 11, श्लोक 12)

"Prakriti is the natural state of doshas, while Vikriti is the state of doshic imbalance."

3.2 Synonyms of Prakriti

- **Swabhava:** Refers to the natural state or inherent nature.

- **Vikruti:** Imbalance or deviation from the natural state.

- **Deha Prakriti:** Physical constitution.

- **Manasa Prakriti:** Mental constitution.

Chapter 4

Intra-uterine Factors Influencing Deha-Prakriti

4.1 Maternal Factors

- **Diet and Lifestyle:** The mother's diet and lifestyle during pregnancy significantly influence the developing fetus's Prakriti.

- **Emotional State:** The emotional well-being of the mother impacts the psychological traits of the child.

- **Age of Parents:** The age of both parents at the time of conception affects the Prakriti of the offspring.

मातुः प्रकृतिरेवात्र गर्भेण सह कृत्स्नशः। आहार-विहारोक्तं च यन्मातुर्निर्दिश्यते॥

(चरक संहिता, शारीर स्थान, अध्याय 4, श्लोक 36)

"The mother's Prakriti, along with her diet and lifestyle, entirely influences the fetus."

4.2 Genetic Factors

- **Inherited Traits:** Genetic predisposition plays a crucial role in determining an individual's Prakriti.

- **Parental Prakriti:** The combined Prakriti of both parents contributes to the child's constitution.

4.3 Environmental Factors

- **Season and Climate:** The season and climate at the time of conception and during pregnancy influence the formation of Prakriti.

- **Geographical Location:** The region where the mother resides during pregnancy affects the fetus's development.

कालो देशश्च मातुश्च विकारश्चानुलोमनः। जातः संयोगजं कारणं विकृतिमेव च॥

(सुश्रुत संहिता, शारीर स्थान, अध्याय 3, श्लोक 17)

"Time, place, and the mother's condition, along with genetic factors, contribute to the formation of Prakriti."

Chapter 5

Extra-uterine Factors Influencing Deha-Prakriti

5.1 Postnatal Environment

- **Diet and Nutrition:** The type of food consumed during infancy and childhood affects Prakriti.

- **Lifestyle:** Physical activity, sleep patterns, and daily routines influence the expression of Prakriti.

- **Exposure to Environmental Toxins:** Contact with pollutants and toxins can impact the natural constitution.

आहारविहाराणां संयोगानामनुत्तमान्। प्रकृतिं विकृतिं चैव भेषजं चोपधारयेत्॥

(चरक संहिता, सूत्र स्थान, अध्याय 1, श्लोक 54)

"Food and lifestyle habits determine the natural constitution, its imbalances, and remedies."

5.2 Psychological Factors

- **Emotional Experiences:** Childhood experiences and emotional well-being shape the mental aspect of Prakriti.

- **Parental Influence:** The attitudes and behaviors of parents and caregivers contribute to the development of Manasa-Prakriti.

Chapter 6

Classification of Deha-Prakriti

6.1 Vata Prakriti

वायोः प्रकृतिः शीघ्रता चलता लघुता स्थिता। स्थैर्यमुद्योगिनः शीघ्रं विकारं गच्छति ध्रुवम्॥

(चरक संहिता, सूत्र स्थान, अध्याय 18, श्लोक 50)

"The nature of Vata is speed, movement, lightness, and instability, leading to quick changes and imbalances."

6.2 Pitta Prakriti

पित्तस्य प्रकृतिः तीक्ष्णोष्णं द्रवमम्लं कटुकं लघु। तेजोवतेश्च विज्ञेयाः पित्तप्रकृतयः॥

(सुश्रुत संहिता, सूत्र स्थान, अध्याय 15, श्लोक 5)

"The nature of Pitta is sharp, hot, liquid, sour, pungent, and light, indicative of fiery characteristics."

6.3 Kapha Prakriti

कफस्य प्रकृतिः शीतं गुरु मन्दं स्निग्धं श्लक्ष्णं स्थिरं मृदु। प्रसन्नं च च स्वभावतः प्रकृतिमुपगच्छति॥

(चरक संहिता, सूत्र स्थान, अध्याय 12, श्लोक 9)

"The nature of Kapha is cold, heavy, slow, oily, smooth, stable, and soft, contributing to a calm disposition."

6.4 Dual and Triple Dosha Prakriti

- **Vata-Pitta:** Combination of Vata and Pitta characteristics.

- **Pitta-Kapha:** Combination of Pitta and Kapha traits.

- **Vata-Kapha:** Combination of Vata and Kapha features.

- **Sama Prakriti:** Balanced state of all three doshas.

Chapter 7

Characteristic Features of Each Kind of Deha-Prakriti

7.1 Vata Prakriti

Physical Traits:

- Slender build

- Dry skin

- Cold extremities

Mental Traits:

- Creativity

- Quick thinking

- Nervousness

Health Tendencies:

- Prone to anxiety

- Insomnia

- Digestive issues

वायोः प्रकृतिरूक्षत्वं लाघवमचलत्वता। क्षणिकत्वे च संयुक्ता विकारांश्च प्रदर्शयेत्॥

(अष्टांग हृदय, सूत्र स्थान, अध्याय 12, श्लोक 1)

"The nature of Vata is roughness, lightness, and instability, showing symptoms of quick changes and imbalances."

7.2 Pitta Prakriti

Physical Traits:

- Moderate build

- Warm body

- Prone to rashes

Mental Traits:

- Intelligence

- Determination

- Irritability

Health Tendencies:

- Susceptible to inflammation

- Acidity

- Skin disorders

पित्तस्य प्रकृतिः तीक्ष्णा उष्णा द्रवा लघुः। तस्मे चलति संवेगात् विकारं प्राप्य निश्चितम्॥

(अष्टांग हृदय, सूत्र स्थान, अध्याय 12, श्लोक 2)

"The nature of Pitta is sharp, hot, and light, causing quick changes and imbalances."

7.3 Kapha Prakriti

Physical Traits:

- Sturdy build

- Oily skin

- Slow metabolism

Mental Traits:

- Calmness

- Loyalty

- Lethargy

Health Tendencies:

- Prone to weight gain

- Respiratory issues

- Depression

कफस्य प्रकृतिः स्निग्धं शीतं गुरु मृदु। स्थिरं मन्दं च संयुक्तं विकारं प्राप्य यत्नतः॥

(अष्टांग हृदय, सूत्र स्थान, अध्याय 12, श्लोक 3)

"The nature of Kapha is oily, cold, heavy, and stable, causing slow changes and imbalances."

7.4 Dual and Triple Dosha Prakriti

- **Vata-Pitta:** Combination of creativity and determination, prone to digestive issues and stress.

- **Pitta-Kapha:** Mix of intelligence and stability, susceptible to inflammatory and respiratory conditions.

- **Vata-Kapha:** Blend of agility and calmness, prone to joint problems and weight fluctuations.

- **Sama Prakriti:** Balanced constitution with optimal health, less prone to diseases.

Chapter 8

Introduction to Manasa-Prakriti

8.1 Definition and Concept

Manasa-Prakriti refers to the mental constitution of an individual, determined by the balance of the three Gunas: Sattva, Rajas, and Tamas. It shapes one's psychological traits, behaviors, and emotional responses.

8.2 Historical Perspective

The concept of Manasa-Prakriti has been discussed in Ayurvedic texts to emphasize the importance of mental health in overall well-being. Ancient sages identified the influence of mental constitution on physical health and vice versa.

सत्त्वं रजस्तमश्चेति गुणा बुद्ध्युपलक्षणाः। विवृद्धा विवृणोति हि यदृच्छावशतो गुणाः॥

(चरक संहिता, शारीर स्थान, अध्याय 4, श्लोक 37)

"Sattva, Rajas, and Tamas are the three Gunas that define the mind. They vary in influence according to circumstances."

Chapter 9

Types of Manasa-Prakriti

9.1 Sattvika Prakriti

Characteristics:

- Calmness

- Clarity

- Wisdom

- Compassion

Health Tendencies:

- Good mental health

- Strong immunity

- Balanced emotions

सत्त्वं स्वभावतः शुद्धं यद्विशुद्धे तु तद्ध्रुवम्। तत्त्रायते नापथ्येभ्यो मनःशुद्धिं तु सत्त्ववम्॥

(अष्टांग हृदय, शारीर स्थान, अध्याय 1, श्लोक 28)

"Sattva is naturally pure, leading to mental clarity and protecting the mind from harmful influences."

9.2 Rajasika Prakriti

Characteristics:

- Activity

- Ambition

- Restlessness

- Passion

Health Tendencies:

- Prone to stress

- Anxiety

- Digestive issues

रजो रागात्मकं विद्धि तृष्णासङ्गसमुद्भवम्। निबध्नाति सत्त्वं सङ्गेन हन्ति च विशुद्धि तम्॥

(अष्टांग हृदय, शारीर स्थान, अध्याय 1, श्लोक 29)

"Rajas is characterized by passion and activity, causing attachment and agitation."

9.3 Tamasika Prakriti

Characteristics:

- Inertia

- Confusion

- Lethargy

- Ignorance

Health Tendencies:

- Susceptible to depression

- Obesity

- Chronic illnesses

तमस्त्वज्ञानजं विद्धि मोहनं सर्वदेहिनाम्। प्रमादालस्यनिद्राभिः तन्निबध्नाति भारत॥

(अष्टांग हृदय, शारीर स्थान, अध्याय 1, श्लोक 30)

"Tamas is born from ignorance, causing delusion, laziness, and sleep."

9.4 Mixed Manasa-Prakriti

- **Sattva-Rajas:** Blend of calmness and activity, prone to occasional stress.

- **Rajas-Tamas:** Combination of restlessness and lethargy, susceptible to mood swings.

- **Sattva-Tamas:** Mix of wisdom and inertia, prone to confusion and indecision.

Anukatva (Animal Analogies)

2.2 Animal Analogies for Vata Prakriti

1. Donkey: Donkeys are often restless, agile, and resilient, which are characteristic traits of Vata individuals. They are known for their endurance and ability to move swiftly.

2. Deer: Deer are light, quick, and always alert, reflecting the lightness, mobility, and nervous energy associated with Vata dosha.

3. Monkey: Monkeys exhibit rapid movements, agility, and high energy levels, making them an excellent analogy for Vata Prakriti. Their curious and playful nature also mirrors the creative and enthusiastic aspects of Vata.

Chapter 10

Pitta Prakriti: Characteristics and Animal Analogies

3.1 Characteristics of Pitta Prakriti

Pitta dosha is primarily composed of Fire and Water, representing transformation and metabolism. Its key characteristics include:

- **Ushna (Hot)**

- **Tikshna (Sharp)**

- **Sara (Flowing)**

- **Drava (Liquid)**

- **Amla (Sour)**

- **Laghu (Light)**

पित्तस्य प्रकृतिः तीक्ष्णोष्णं द्रवमम्लं कटुकं लघु। तेजोवतेश्च विज्ञेयाः पित्तप्रकृतयः॥

(सुश्रुत संहिता, सूत्र स्थान, अध्याय 15, श्लोक 5)

"The nature of Pitta is sharp, hot, liquid, sour, pungent, and light, indicative of fiery characteristics."

3.2 Animal Analogies for Pitta Prakriti

1. Lion: Lions are strong, courageous, and dominant, reflecting the intense and fiery nature of Pitta individuals. Their leadership and competitive spirit are also characteristic of Pitta dosha.

2. Eagle: Eagles are sharp, focused, and have a keen vision, which aligns with the sharpness, intelligence, and clarity associated with Pitta Prakriti.

3. Tiger: Tigers exhibit strength, agility, and a powerful presence, embodying the fiery and dynamic aspects of Pitta dosha. Their intense gaze and strategic hunting methods reflect the determined and precise nature of Pitta individuals.

Chapter 11

Kapha Prakriti: Characteristics and Animal Analogies

4.1 Characteristics of Kapha Prakriti

Kapha dosha is primarily composed of Water and Earth, representing stability and structure. Its key characteristics include:

- **Guru (Heavy)**

- **Manda (Slow)**

- **Sheeta (Cold)**

- **Snigdha (Unctuous)**

- **Shlakshna (Smooth)**

- **Sthira (Stable)**

- **Madhura (Sweet)**

कफस्य प्रकृतिः शीतं गुरु मन्दं स्निग्धं श्लक्ष्णं स्थिरं मृदु। प्रसन्नं च च स्वभावतः प्रकृतिमुपगच्छति॥

(चरक संहिता, सूत्र स्थान, अध्याय 12, श्लोक 9)

"The nature of Kapha is cold, heavy, slow, oily, smooth, stable, and soft, contributing to a calm disposition."

4.2 Animal Analogies for Kapha Prakriti

1. Elephant: Elephants are large, stable, and have a calm demeanor, which mirrors the grounded and steady nature of Kapha individuals. Their strength and endurance also reflect the robustness associated with Kapha dosha.

2. Cow: Cows are gentle, nurturing, and possess a serene presence, aligning with the nurturing, patient, and compassionate qualities of Kapha Prakriti.

3. Turtle: Turtles move slowly and steadily, symbolizing the slow, stable, and resilient characteristics of Kapha dosha. Their protective shell also represents the protective and supportive nature of Kapha individuals.

Chapter -12

Ayurgenomics

Ayurgenomics is a field that integrates the ancient wisdom of *Ayurveda* with modern genomics. It aims to provide a deeper understanding of individual variability in health and disease by connecting the personalized concepts of *Ayurveda* (such as *Prakriti*) with the emerging science of genomics. This approach blends traditional knowledge of human constitution and lifestyle factors with advanced genetic and molecular tools to offer personalized healthcare.

1. Concept of *Prakriti* in Ayurveda: In *Ayurveda*, *Prakriti* refers to the natural constitution of an individual, which is determined by the predominance of three *Doshas—Vata*, *Pitta*, and *Kapha*. Each person's *Prakriti* is believed to be established at conception and remains stable throughout life. It influences an individual's physical characteristics, mental behavior, susceptibility to diseases, and responses to treatments.

The classification of *Prakriti* is broadly divided into seven categories based on the dominance of one or more *Doshas*:

- *Vata Prakriti*

- *Pitta Prakriti*

- *Kapha Prakriti*

- *Vata-Pitta Prakriti* (Dual)

- *Pitta-Kapha Prakriti* (Dual)

- *Vata-Kapha Prakriti* (Dual)

- *Sama Prakriti* (Balanced)

Each type of *Prakriti* exhibits distinct characteristics, and this influences a person's predisposition to certain diseases and their responses to diet, lifestyle, and therapies.

2. Genomics: Genomics is the branch of molecular biology concerned with the structure, function, evolution, and mapping of genomes. A genome is the complete set of genes or genetic material present in a cell or organism. Genomics focuses on the interaction between these genes and how they regulate physiological processes and influence susceptibility to diseases.

With the advent of high-throughput sequencing technologies, researchers can now explore the genetic makeup of individuals and identify variations that contribute to their unique health profiles.

3. Integration of Ayurveda and Genomics: The concept of *Ayurgenomics* emerged as an attempt to validate and expand *Ayurveda's* personalized approach using modern genetic insights. This integration aims to identify correlations between *Prakriti* classifications and genetic markers, thereby providing a scientific basis for *Ayurveda's* principles of personalized healthcare.

Several research studies have shown that individuals with different *Prakriti* types exhibit specific genetic and molecular signatures that correspond to their physical and mental traits. For instance:

- *Vata Prakriti* individuals may show gene variations associated with neurotransmitter regulation, contributing to their traits of creativity, enthusiasm, and adaptability.

- *Pitta Prakriti* individuals may exhibit variations in genes linked to metabolism and inflammatory processes, aligning with their tendency toward heat, sharpness, and decisiveness.

- *Kapha Prakriti* individuals might have genetic traits associated with anabolic processes, aligning with their heavier build, endurance, and calm temperament.

4. Genomic Correlates of *Prakriti*: Ayurgenomics research has identified links between specific genetic polymorphisms and *Prakriti*. For example:

- Variations in the **CYP2C19** gene have been associated with differences in drug metabolism across different *Prakriti* types.

- **HLA (Human Leukocyte Antigen)** genes, which play a role in the immune response, have been found to correlate with *Prakriti* types, suggesting that each *Prakriti* may have a distinct immune profile.

5. Benefits of Ayurgenomics:

1. **Personalized Medicine:** Ayurgenomics provides a framework for developing highly personalized medical treatments based on an individual's *Prakriti* and genetic makeup. This can lead to more effective therapies and better patient outcomes.

2. **Preventive Healthcare:** By understanding a person's *Prakriti* and genetic susceptibilities, preventive strategies can be designed to mitigate the risk of developing specific diseases. For instance, individuals with a *Pitta Prakriti* may be more prone to inflammatory disorders, and lifestyle modifications can be suggested to prevent such conditions.

3. **Pharmacogenomics:** Ayurgenomics enhances pharmacogenomics by predicting how an individual might respond to drugs based on both their genetic profile and their *Prakriti*. This can reduce adverse drug reactions and optimize therapeutic efficacy.

4. **Holistic Approach:** While genomics provides insights at the molecular level, *Ayurveda* takes into account the broader context of lifestyle, environment, and mental health. Ayurgenomics bridges this gap, offering a more holistic view of health.

6. Ayurgenomics in Disease Management: Ayurgenomics has the potential to revolutionize disease management by providing tailored interventions. For instance, conditions like diabetes, cardiovascular diseases, and cancer show distinct correlations with both genetic markers and *Prakriti* types.

- **Diabetes:** Studies have shown that individuals with *Kapha Prakriti* are more susceptible to type 2 diabetes. Genomic analysis has further identified polymorphisms in genes related to insulin resistance that align with this predisposition.

- **Cardiovascular Diseases:** *Pitta Prakriti* individuals are believed to be more prone to inflammatory conditions and cardiovascular diseases. Genomic studies have supported this by identifying specific markers associated with increased inflammation in these individuals.

- **Mental Health:** *Vata Prakriti* individuals may have a higher predisposition to anxiety and nervous system disorders, which may correspond to variations in genes regulating neurotransmitters.

7. Current Research and Future Directions: Research in Ayurgenomics is still in its early stages, but promising results have already been observed. Ongoing projects like the **CSIR-Trisutra Project** aim to decode the genetic basis of *Prakriti* and develop diagnostic tools for personalized medicine.

Future research could explore:

- **Epigenetics and Prakriti:** Understanding how environmental factors influence gene expression across different *Prakriti* types.

- **Microbiome Research:** Investigating how the gut microbiome varies across *Prakriti* types and influences health.

- **Genetic Counseling:** Developing guidelines for genetic counseling based on *Ayurvedic* principles and genomic insights.

Chapter 13

Human Genomics

Human Genomics: A Comprehensive Textbook

Table of Contents

1. Introduction to Human Genomics

2. History and Evolution of Genomic Studies

3. Structure and Function of DNA

4. The Human Genome Project

5. Genomic Technologies and Methodologies

6. Genetic Variation and Mutation

7. Genomics in Medicine

8. Ethical, Legal, and Social Implications of Genomics

9. Future Directions in Human Genomics

10. Case Studies in Human Genomics

Chapter 14

Introduction to Human Genomics

1.1 Definition and Scope

Human Genomics Defined

Human genomics is a branch of biology focused on the study of the genome – the complete set of DNA within a single human cell. The genome comprises approximately 3 billion base pairs of DNA, containing about 20,000-25,000 genes. These genes encode the instructions necessary for the structure, function, and regulation of the body's cells, tissues, and organs. Beyond the coding regions, the genome also includes non-coding regions that play critical roles in gene regulation and genome stability.

Scope of Human Genomics

The scope of human genomics extends beyond the mere cataloging of genes to encompass a broader understanding of how genes function and interact:

1. **Gene Structure and Function:** This includes studying the physical arrangement of genes within the genome, their roles in coding for proteins, and how they are regulated.

2. **Genetic Variation:** Understanding the variations in the DNA sequence among individuals, which can influence traits, susceptibility to diseases, and responses to treatments.

3. **Gene-Gene Interactions:** Exploring how different genes interact with each other to affect biological pathways and processes.

4. **Gene-Environment Interactions:** Investigating how environmental factors such as diet, lifestyle, and exposure to toxins interact with genetic makeup to influence

health and disease.

5. **Epigenetics:** Studying heritable changes in gene expression that do not involve changes to the underlying DNA sequence, often influenced by environmental factors.

Applications of Genomics

The insights from genomics research have vast applications across various fields:

- **Medicine:** Identifying genetic factors underlying diseases, leading to improved diagnostics, targeted therapies, and personalized medicine.

- **Pharmacogenomics:** Understanding how genetic variations affect drug metabolism and efficacy, enabling personalized drug prescriptions.

- **Forensics:** Using genetic information for identification in legal cases.

- **Anthropology and Evolution:** Tracing human evolution and migration patterns through genetic analysis.

- **Agriculture:** Enhancing crop and livestock breeding through genetic insights.

1.2 Importance of Genomics

Advancing Medical Research

Human genomics has revolutionized medical research by providing a comprehensive understanding of the genetic basis of diseases. Researchers can now identify genetic mutations associated with specific diseases, understand disease mechanisms, and develop targeted therapies. For example:

- **Cancer Genomics:** By identifying mutations in cancer cells, researchers have developed targeted therapies that specifically attack cancer cells without harming normal cells.

- **Cardiovascular Diseases:** Genetic research has identified genes associated with heart diseases, leading to better prevention strategies and treatments.

Improving Disease Diagnosis and Treatment

Genomics has led to the development of genetic tests that can diagnose diseases more accurately and earlier than traditional methods. For instance:

- **Genetic Testing:** Tests for conditions like cystic fibrosis, Huntington's disease, and hereditary cancers allow for early diagnosis and intervention.

- **Pharmacogenomics:** Genetic information guides the choice of drugs and dosages, reducing adverse drug reactions and improving treatment efficacy.

Personalized Medicine

One of the most significant impacts of genomics is the shift towards personalized medicine, where treatments and preventive strategies are tailored to an individual's genetic profile. Personalized medicine considers:

- **Genetic Predisposition:** Identifying individuals at high risk for certain diseases allows for personalized prevention plans.

- **Tailored Therapies:** Treatments based on a person's genetic makeup can be more effective and have fewer side effects. For example, BRCA gene testing in breast cancer helps determine the best preventive or therapeutic measures.

Understanding Human Biology and Evolution

Genomics provides insights into human biology and the evolutionary history of our species:

- **Gene Function and Regulation:** Understanding how genes work and are regulated helps elucidate biological processes and disease mechanisms.

- **Human Evolution:** Genomic studies trace the evolutionary history of humans, identifying how genetic diversity has shaped populations over time.

Impact on Society

The benefits of human genomics extend to society at large, influencing various aspects such as:

- **Public Health:** Genomic information can inform public health strategies to manage and prevent diseases.

- **Ethical Considerations:** The application of genomics raises ethical issues related to privacy, genetic discrimination, and access to genetic information. It is crucial to address these concerns to ensure the responsible use of genomic data.

Chapter 15

History and Evolution of Genomic Studies

2.1 Early Discoveries in Genetics

Gregor Mendel's Work

Gregor Mendel, an Austrian monk, is known as the "father of genetics" due to his groundbreaking experiments on inheritance patterns in pea plants conducted in the mid-19th century. Mendel's work, published in 1866, laid the foundation for modern genetics. His key discoveries included:

1. **Law of Segregation:** Each individual has two alleles for each gene, which segregate during the formation of gametes (sperm and eggs), ensuring that each gamete contains only one allele.

2. **Law of Independent Assortment:** Genes for different traits segregate independently of one another during gamete formation.

Mendel's principles were not recognized until the early 20th century when they were rediscovered by scientists Hugo de Vries, Carl Correns, and Erich von Tschermak. Mendel's meticulous work provided the basis for understanding how traits are inherited from one generation to the next.

Discovery of DNA Structure

The discovery of the DNA structure in 1953 by James Watson and Francis Crick was a pivotal moment in genetics. Their model of the DNA double helix revealed:

1. **Double Helix Structure:** DNA consists of two strands that coil around each other, forming a double helix.

2. **Base Pairing:** Adenine (A) pairs with thymine (T), and cytosine (C) pairs with guanine

(G) through hydrogen bonds. This base-pairing mechanism is crucial for the replication and transmission of genetic information.

3. **Genetic Information Storage:** The sequence of the four nucleotide bases (A, T, C, G) along the DNA strand encodes the genetic instructions necessary for the development and functioning of living organisms.

This discovery was based on the X-ray diffraction images produced by Rosalind Franklin and Maurice Wilkins, as well as the base composition studies of Erwin Chargaff. The double helix model provided critical insights into how genetic information is stored, replicated, and transmitted.

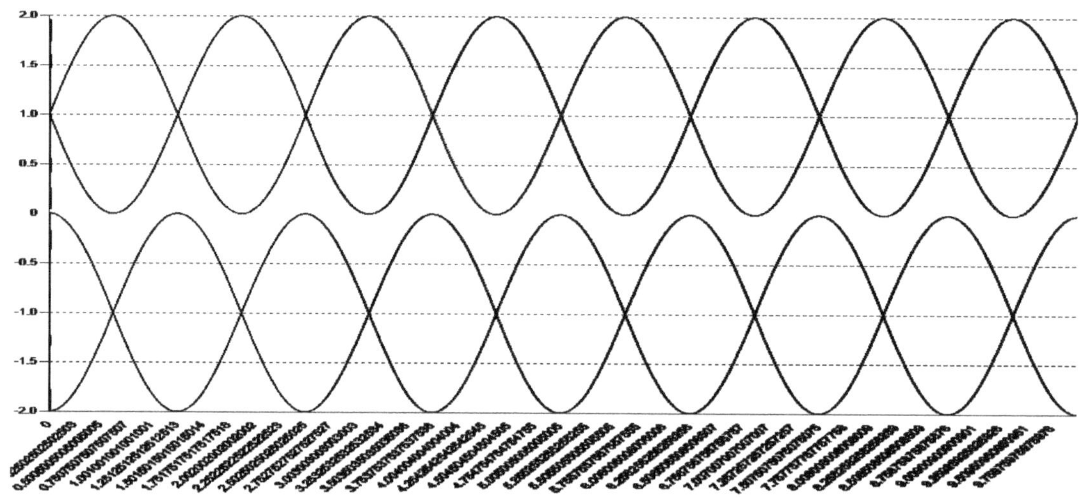

2.2 Milestones in Genomics

Development of Sequencing Technologies

The advent of DNA sequencing technologies in the late 20th century revolutionized the field of genomics:

1. **Sanger Sequencing (1977):** Developed by Frederick Sanger, this method involves the use of chain-terminating nucleotides to determine the sequence of DNA. It became the gold standard for DNA sequencing for several decades and allowed scientists to sequence longer DNA fragments accurately.

2. **Next-Generation Sequencing (NGS):** Emerging in the early 21st century, NGS

technologies such as Illumina sequencing and pyrosequencing allowed the high-throughput sequencing of millions of DNA fragments simultaneously. NGS significantly reduced the cost and time required for sequencing, making large-scale genomic studies feasible.

3. **Third-Generation Sequencing Technologies:** Techniques like single-molecule real-time (SMRT) sequencing and nanopore sequencing provide longer read lengths and real-time analysis, further advancing the field of genomics.

Chapter -16

The Human Genome Project (HGP)

The Human Genome Project (HGP) was an ambitious international endeavor to map and sequence the entire human genome. Initiated in 1990 and completed in 2003, the HGP aimed to identify all human genes and understand their functions.

Objectives and Goals:

1. **Complete Sequencing:** Sequence the entire human genome, encompassing approximately 3 billion base pairs.

2. **Gene Identification:** Identify all human genes, estimated to be around 20,000-25,000.

3. **Data Availability:** Make the genomic data freely accessible to researchers worldwide.

4. **Technological Advancements:** Develop new technologies and methodologies for genomic analysis.

5. **Ethical Considerations:** Address the ethical, legal, and social implications of genomic research.

Major Achievements:

1. **Draft Sequence (2000):** The first draft of the human genome was completed, covering 90% of the genome with 99.9% accuracy.

2. **Completion (2003):** The finished sequence covered 99% of the genome with less than 1 error per 10,000 base pairs.

3. **Reference Genome:** Provided a reference genome for further research, facilitating

the identification of genetic variations and their association with diseases.

Impact on Science and Medicine:

- **Disease Understanding:** Enabled the identification of genes associated with various diseases, leading to improved diagnostics and targeted therapies.

- **Personalized Medicine:** Paved the way for personalized medicine, where treatments are tailored to an individual's genetic profile.

- **Biotechnological Advances:** Spurred the development of new technologies and bioinformatics tools for genomic research.

Table 2.1: Key Milestones in the Human Genome Project

Year	Milestone
1990	Initiation of the Human Genome Project
1996	Yeast genome sequenced
1998	Caenorhabditis elegans genome sequenced
2000	Draft sequence of the human genome completed
2001	First analysis papers published in Nature and Science
2003	Completion of the Human Genome Project

Chapter 16

Structure and Function of DNA

3.1 DNA Structure

DNA (deoxyribonucleic acid) is the molecule that carries the genetic instructions for life. The structure of DNA is essential for its function in storing and transmitting genetic information. It is composed of two strands forming a double helix.

Structure:

1. **Double Helix:**

   - The DNA molecule is structured as a double helix, which resembles a twisted ladder.

   - Each strand of the helix is composed of a long chain of nucleotides.

2. **Sugar-Phosphate Backbone:**

   - Each nucleotide in the DNA strand consists of a phosphate group, a sugar molecule (deoxyribose), and a nitrogenous base.

   - The phosphate group of one nucleotide bonds with the sugar molecule of the next nucleotide, creating a sugar-phosphate backbone for each strand.

   - These backbones run in opposite directions (antiparallel), one in the 5' to 3' direction and the other in the 3' to 5' direction.

3. **Nitrogenous Bases:**

   - There are four types of nitrogenous bases in DNA: adenine (A), thymine (T), cytosine (C), and guanine (G).

- o The bases attach to the sugar molecules of the backbone and extend inward toward the center of the helix.

4. **Base Pairing:**

- o The two strands are held together by hydrogen bonds between the nitrogenous bases.

- o Adenine (A) pairs with thymine (T) through two hydrogen bonds, and cytosine (C) pairs with guanine (G) through three hydrogen bonds.

- o This complementary base pairing is crucial for the accurate replication of DNA and for maintaining the genetic code.

Function:

The double helix structure of DNA allows it to store genetic information in a compact and stable form. The specific sequence of bases encodes genetic instructions, which are essential for the synthesis of proteins and the regulation of cellular activities.

3.2 Gene Structure

Genes are the functional units of DNA that contain the instructions for synthesizing proteins and functional RNA molecules. A gene is composed of several regions that contribute to its function.

Structure:

1. **Exons:**

- o Exons are the coding regions of a gene that contain the information required to synthesize proteins.

- o During gene expression, exons are transcribed into messenger RNA (mRNA) and then translated into proteins.

2. **Introns:**

- o Introns are non-coding regions interspersed between exons.

o Introns are transcribed into pre-mRNA but are removed during RNA splicing to produce mature mRNA.

3. **Regulatory Elements:**

   o **Promoters:** Sequences located upstream of the coding region that provide binding sites for RNA polymerase and transcription factors, initiating transcription.

   o **Enhancers:** Sequences that can increase the transcription of a gene, often located far from the gene they regulate.

   o **Silencers:** Sequences that can suppress the transcription of a gene.

   o **Terminators:** Sequences that signal the end of transcription.

Function:

Genes are responsible for the production of proteins, which perform various structural, enzymatic, and regulatory roles in the cell. The regulatory elements ensure that genes are expressed at the right time, place, and amount, allowing for precise control over cellular functions.

3.3 DNA Replication and Repair

DNA replication is the process by which a DNA molecule is copied to produce two identical DNA molecules. This is essential for cell division and the transmission of genetic information from one generation to the next. DNA repair mechanisms correct errors that occur during replication and protect against mutations.

Detailed Process:

1. **DNA Replication:**

   o **Semi-Conservative Replication:** Each new DNA molecule consists of one old (parental) strand and one new (daughter) strand.

   o **Initiation:** Replication begins at specific locations called origins of replication, where the DNA double helix is unwound by helicase enzymes.

- o **Elongation:** DNA polymerase enzymes add complementary nucleotides to each template strand, synthesizing new DNA strands.

- o **Termination:** Replication ends when the entire DNA molecule has been copied, resulting in two identical DNA molecules.

2. **DNA Repair Mechanisms:**

- o **Nucleotide Excision Repair (NER):** Repairs bulky lesions, such as thymine dimers, caused by UV radiation. NER removes a short single-stranded DNA segment containing the damage and fills in the gap with newly synthesized DNA.

- o **Base Excision Repair (BER):** Repairs small, non-helix-distorting base lesions. BER removes the damaged base, leaving an abasic site, which is then filled in with the correct nucleotide.

- o **Mismatch Repair (MMR):** Corrects base-pairing mismatches that escape proofreading during replication. MMR identifies the mismatch, removes the incorrect nucleotide, and fills in the gap with the correct one.

- o **Homologous Recombination (HR):** Repairs double-strand breaks by using a homologous sequence as a template for accurate repair.

- o **Non-Homologous End Joining (NHEJ):** Repairs double-strand breaks by directly joining the broken ends, often leading to insertions or deletions.

Function:

DNA replication ensures that each daughter cell receives an identical copy of the DNA during cell division. DNA repair mechanisms maintain the integrity of the genetic information by correcting errors that occur during replication and protecting against mutations that can lead to diseases, such as cancer.

Chapter 17

The Human Genome Project

4.1 Objectives and Goals

The Human Genome Project (HGP) was an ambitious international initiative that aimed to map and sequence the entire human genome. Launched in 1990 and completed in 2003, the HGP had several primary objectives and goals:

1. **Mapping the Human Genome:**

   - Create a comprehensive map of the human genome, detailing the location of every gene on the 23 pairs of human chromosomes.

   - Identify the precise locations and sequences of the genes within the genome.

2. **Sequencing the Human Genome:**

   - Determine the complete nucleotide sequence of the human genome's approximately 3 billion base pairs.

   - Develop accurate and efficient sequencing techniques to achieve this goal.

3. **Identifying All Human Genes:**

   - Catalog all the genes in the human genome, estimated to be around 20,000-25,000 protein-coding genes.

   - Understand the structure, function, and organization of these genes.

4. **Understanding Gene Function:**

   - Investigate the functions of identified genes and their roles in health and disease.

   - Study how genes interact with each other and with environmental factors to influence biological processes.

5. **Developing Genomic Technologies:**

   o Foster the development of new technologies and computational tools to analyze and interpret genomic data.

   o Improve the accuracy, speed, and cost-effectiveness of DNA sequencing and analysis.

6. **Addressing Ethical, Legal, and Social Implications (ELSI):**

   o Explore the ethical, legal, and social issues arising from genomic research.

   o Ensure that genomic information is used responsibly and ethically.

7. **Promoting International Collaboration:**

   o Encourage cooperation among researchers, institutions, and countries to share data and resources.

   o Facilitate open access to genomic information for the global scientific community.

4.2 Major Achievements

The Human Genome Project achieved several significant milestones during its course, leading to groundbreaking discoveries and advancements:

1. **Complete Reference Sequence:**

   • The HGP produced a complete reference sequence of the human genome, covering approximately 99% of the genome with high accuracy.

   • This reference sequence serves as a foundational resource for genetic research and clinical applications.

2. **Gene Identification:**

   • The project identified the locations and sequences of all human genes, providing a comprehensive catalog of protein-coding genes.

- This information has been crucial for understanding gene function and regulation.

3. **Technological Advancements:**

   - The HGP spurred the development of innovative sequencing technologies, such as next-generation sequencing (NGS), which have revolutionized genomic research.

   - Advances in bioinformatics and computational tools have enabled efficient analysis and interpretation of large-scale genomic data.

4. **Genetic Basis of Diseases:**

   - The project provided insights into the genetic basis of numerous diseases, including cancer, cardiovascular diseases, and neurological disorders.

   - Identifying disease-associated genes has paved the way for improved diagnostics, targeted therapies, and personalized medicine.

5. **Resource for Further Research:**

   - The genomic data generated by the HGP has become a vital resource for researchers worldwide.

   - It has facilitated the discovery of new genes, genetic variations, and their roles in health and disease.

4.3 Impact on Science and Medicine

The Human Genome Project has had a profound impact on science and medicine, transforming biomedical research and clinical practice in several ways:

1. **Discovery of Disease-Associated Genes:**

   - The identification of genes associated with various diseases has enhanced our understanding of the molecular mechanisms underlying these conditions.

o   This knowledge has led to the development of genetic tests for early diagnosis and risk assessment.

2. **Advancement of Personalized Medicine:**

o   The HGP has paved the way for personalized medicine, where treatments and preventive strategies are tailored to an individual's genetic makeup.

o   Pharmacogenomics, the study of how genes influence drug response, has enabled the customization of drug therapies to improve efficacy and reduce adverse effects.

3. **Development of New Therapeutics:**

o   Insights gained from the HGP have facilitated the development of targeted therapies, such as gene therapy and molecularly targeted drugs.

o   These therapies aim to correct genetic defects or inhibit specific molecular pathways involved in disease progression.

4. **International Collaboration and Data Sharing:**

o   The HGP fostered unprecedented international collaboration, bringing together researchers from various countries to share data and resources.

o   The open access to genomic data has accelerated scientific discoveries and innovations.

5. **Ethical, Legal, and Social Considerations:**

o   The HGP has highlighted the importance of addressing ethical, legal, and social issues related to genomic research.

o   It has prompted discussions on privacy, informed consent, genetic discrimination, and equitable access to genomic technologies.

Chapter 18

Genomic Technologies and Methodologies

5.1 DNA Sequencing Technologies

The advancement of DNA sequencing technologies has been crucial for the rapid progress in genomics. Various sequencing methods have been developed over the years, each with its own advantages and limitations.

Sanger Sequencing

Sanger sequencing, developed by Frederick Sanger in 1977, was the first widely used DNA sequencing method. It is also known as the chain-termination method.

Methodology:

1. **DNA Fragmentation:**

   - The DNA to be sequenced is fragmented into smaller pieces.

   - These fragments are used as templates for sequencing.

2. **Chain Termination:**

   - The DNA fragments are amplified using polymerase chain reaction (PCR).

   - During PCR, a mixture of normal deoxynucleotides (dNTPs) and dideoxynucleotides (ddNTPs) is used.

   - The ddNTPs are chain-terminating nucleotides, meaning once they are incorporated into the growing DNA strand, the elongation stops.

   - Each ddNTP is labeled with a distinct fluorescent dye corresponding to one of the four bases (A, T, C, G).

3. **Separation and Detection:**

   o The DNA fragments of different lengths are separated by capillary electrophoresis.

   o The fluorescently labeled ddNTPs are detected by a laser, and the sequence is determined by analyzing the color and position of the terminated fragments.

Applications:

- Sanger sequencing is used for sequencing small DNA fragments and validating results from other sequencing methods.

- It was the primary technology used in the Human Genome Project.

Next-Generation Sequencing (NGS)

Next-Generation Sequencing (NGS) refers to a suite of high-throughput sequencing technologies that allow the simultaneous sequencing of millions of DNA fragments. NGS has revolutionized genomics by providing faster, more accurate, and cost-effective sequencing.

Common NGS Platforms:

1. **Illumina Sequencing:**

   o Uses a sequencing-by-synthesis approach.

   o DNA fragments are attached to a flow cell and amplified to form clusters.

   o Fluorescently labeled nucleotides are incorporated one at a time, and the sequence is determined by capturing images of the fluorescent signals.

2. **Roche 454 Sequencing:**

   o Uses a pyrosequencing approach.

   o DNA fragments are attached to beads and amplified.

   o Nucleotide incorporation is detected by the release of pyrophosphate, which generates a light signal.

3. **Ion Torrent Sequencing:**

   o   Detects the release of hydrogen ions during nucleotide incorporation.

   o   Changes in pH are measured to determine the sequence.

Advantages:

- High-throughput: Can sequence millions of DNA fragments simultaneously.

- Cost-effective: Reduced cost per base compared to Sanger sequencing.

- Versatile: Suitable for a wide range of applications, including whole-genome sequencing, exome sequencing, and transcriptome sequencing.

Third-Generation Sequencing Technologies

Third-generation sequencing technologies provide real-time sequencing of single molecules without the need for PCR amplification. These methods offer longer read lengths and faster sequencing times.

Common Third-Generation Platforms:

1. **Single-Molecule Real-Time (SMRT) Sequencing:**

   o   Developed by Pacific Biosciences (PacBio).

   o   Uses zero-mode waveguides (ZMWs) to observe DNA polymerase activity in real-time.

   o   Incorporation of fluorescently labeled nucleotides is detected as the DNA polymerase synthesizes the complementary strand.

2. **Nanopore Sequencing:**

   o   Developed by Oxford Nanopore Technologies.

   o   DNA molecules are passed through a nanopore embedded in a membrane.

- ○ Changes in electrical current as nucleotides pass through the pore are measured to determine the sequence.

Advantages:

- Long Read Lengths: Capable of reading sequences of several kilobases, which helps in resolving complex genomic regions and structural variants.

- Real-Time Analysis: Provides immediate sequencing results, allowing for rapid decision-making in clinical and research settings.

Applications:

- Whole-genome sequencing of complex organisms.

- Sequencing of repetitive and GC-rich regions.

- Identification of structural variants and epigenetic modifications.

5.2 Bioinformatics Tools

Bioinformatics involves the application of computational tools and techniques to analyze and interpret large volumes of genomic data. The integration of bioinformatics with genomics has revolutionized the field, enabling the efficient processing, storage, and analysis of genetic information.

Key Tools and Applications:

1. **Sequence Alignment Software:**

   - ○ Tools such as BLAST (Basic Local Alignment Search Tool) allow researchers to compare a query sequence against a database of known sequences to identify similarities and functional annotations.

   - ○ BLAST is widely used for identifying homologous genes, predicting functions, and annotating genomes.

2. **Genome Annotation Tools:**

- Genome annotation involves identifying gene locations, coding regions, regulatory elements, and other functional features within a genome.

- Tools like AUGUSTUS and MAKER automate the annotation process, combining evidence from known genes, transcript sequences, and protein databases.

3. **Databases:**

- **GenBank:** A comprehensive public database of nucleotide sequences and supporting bibliographic and biological annotation.

- **Ensembl:** Provides access to a wide range of genomic data, including genome assemblies, gene annotations, comparative genomics, and variation data.

Function:

Bioinformatics tools facilitate the analysis of complex genomic data, enabling researchers to draw meaningful insights from sequencing projects, gene expression studies, and comparative genomics. These tools are essential for advancing our understanding of genetics, disease mechanisms, and evolutionary biology.

5.3 Functional Genomics

Functional genomics aims to understand the roles and interactions of genes and their products within the genome. It encompasses a variety of high-throughput techniques and approaches to study gene expression, protein function, and metabolic pathways.

Key Techniques:

1. **Gene Expression Profiling:**

- **Microarrays:** Utilize a grid of DNA probes to measure the expression levels of thousands of genes simultaneously. Used to compare gene expression between different conditions or treatments.

- **RNA Sequencing (RNA-seq):** Uses next-generation sequencing to capture and quantify the transcriptome. RNA-seq provides detailed information about gene expression levels, alternative splicing events, and non-coding RNA species.

2. **Proteomics:**

   o The large-scale study of proteins, including their structures, functions, and interactions.

   o Techniques such as mass spectrometry (MS) and two-dimensional gel electrophoresis (2D-GE) are used to identify and quantify proteins, analyze post-translational modifications, and study protein-protein interactions.

3. **Metabolomics:**

   o The comprehensive analysis of metabolites within a biological system.

   o Techniques such as nuclear magnetic resonance (NMR) spectroscopy and mass spectrometry are used to profile metabolites and investigate metabolic pathways.

   o Metabolomics provides insights into the biochemical activities and physiological states of cells and tissues.

Applications:

- **Understanding Gene Function:** Functional genomics helps identify the roles of genes and their products in cellular processes and disease mechanisms.

- **Disease Research:** Provides insights into the molecular basis of diseases, identifying potential biomarkers and therapeutic targets.

- **Drug Development:** Assists in the discovery of new drug targets, understanding drug mechanisms, and assessing drug efficacy and toxicity.

- **Systems Biology:** Integrates data from genomics, transcriptomics, proteomics, and metabolomics to build comprehensive models of biological systems.

Chapter 19

Genetic Variation and Mutation

6.1 Types of Genetic Variation

Genetic variation refers to the differences in DNA sequences among individuals within a population. These variations contribute to the uniqueness of each individual and can influence a wide range of traits and susceptibility to diseases.

Types of Genetic Variation:

1. **Single Nucleotide Polymorphisms (SNPs):**

    o   SNPs are the most common type of genetic variation, involving changes at a single nucleotide position in the genome.

    o   A SNP occurs when a single nucleotide (A, T, C, or G) in the DNA sequence is replaced by another nucleotide.

    o   SNPs can occur in coding regions (exons), non-coding regions (introns), or regulatory regions of the genome.

    o   While many SNPs have no effect on health or development, some can influence the risk of developing certain diseases or affect how an individual responds to medications.

2. **Copy Number Variations (CNVs):**

    o   CNVs involve variations in the number of copies of a particular gene or genomic region.

    o   These variations can include duplications (extra copies) or deletions (fewer copies) of genes.

    o   CNVs can have significant effects on gene expression and phenotype, contributing to genetic diversity and susceptibility to diseases.

- o For example, variations in the number of copies of the CCL3L1 gene have been associated with susceptibility to HIV infection.

3. **Structural Variations (SVs):**

- o Structural variations are large-scale alterations in the genome that involve changes in the structure of chromosomes.

- o These variations can include deletions, duplications, inversions, and translocations.

- o Structural variations can have profound effects on gene function and regulation, potentially leading to genetic disorders.

- o For example, a translocation between chromosomes 9 and 22, known as the Philadelphia chromosome, is associated with chronic myeloid leukemia (CML).

6.2 Mechanisms of Mutation

Mutations are changes in the DNA sequence that can occur naturally or be induced by external factors. Mutations can have various effects on gene function, ranging from benign to harmful.

Mechanisms of Mutation:

1. **Spontaneous Mutations:**

- o Spontaneous mutations arise naturally during DNA replication or as a result of spontaneous chemical changes in DNA.

- o These mutations can occur due to errors in DNA replication, spontaneous base modifications, or the insertion of transposable elements.

- o Spontaneous mutations are relatively rare due to the high fidelity of DNA replication and the presence of proofreading mechanisms.

2. **Induced Mutations:**

- o Induced mutations are caused by external factors, such as radiation, chemicals, and viruses.

- o **Radiation:** Exposure to ultraviolet (UV) light, X-rays, or gamma rays can cause DNA damage, leading to mutations.

- o **Chemicals:** Certain chemicals, known as mutagens, can interact with DNA and cause mutations. For example, benzene and aflatoxins are known mutagens.

- o **Viruses:** Some viruses can integrate their genetic material into the host genome, causing mutations and potentially leading to cancer.

DNA Repair Mechanisms:

1. **Mismatch Repair (MMR):**

   - MMR corrects base-pairing mismatches that escape proofreading during DNA replication.

   - The MMR system recognizes and removes the incorrect nucleotide, then fills in the gap with the correct nucleotide.

2. **Homologous Recombination (HR):**

   - HR repairs double-strand breaks using a homologous sequence as a template for accurate repair.

   - This mechanism is crucial for maintaining genomic stability and preventing chromosomal abnormalities.

3. **Nucleotide Excision Repair (NER):**

   - NER repairs bulky lesions, such as thymine dimers, caused by UV radiation.

   - The damaged DNA segment is excised, and the gap is filled in with newly synthesized DNA.

4. **Base Excision Repair (BER):**

- BER repairs small, non-helix-distorting base lesions.

- The damaged base is removed, leaving an abasic site, which is then filled in with the correct nucleotide.

6.3 Impact of Genetic Variation on Phenotype

Genetic variation plays a crucial role in determining individual traits and susceptibility to diseases. The impact of genetic variation on phenotype can be complex, often involving interactions between multiple genes and environmental factors.

Influence on Traits:

1. **Single-Gene Traits:**

   - Some traits are determined by variations in a single gene. These traits typically follow Mendelian inheritance patterns.

   - For example, cystic fibrosis is caused by mutations in the CFTR gene.

2. **Polygenic Traits:**

   - Most traits are influenced by variations in multiple genes, known as polygenic traits.

   - Examples of polygenic traits include height, skin color, and intelligence.

3. **Complex Diseases:**

   - Complex diseases, such as diabetes, heart disease, and cancer, often result from interactions between multiple genetic and environmental factors.

   - Genetic variations can influence an individual's susceptibility to these diseases, as well as their response to treatments.

Environmental Interactions:

1. **Gene-Environment Interactions:**

- Environmental factors, such as diet, lifestyle, and exposure to toxins, can interact with genetic variations to influence phenotype.

- For example, individuals with a genetic predisposition to obesity may be more likely to develop obesity when exposed to a high-calorie diet.

2. **Epigenetics:**

- Epigenetic modifications, such as DNA methylation and histone modification, can influence gene expression without changing the underlying DNA sequence.

- Epigenetic changes can be influenced by environmental factors and can affect an individual's phenotype and disease risk.

Chapter 20

Genomics in Medicine

7.1 Personalized Medicine

Personalized medicine, also known as precision medicine, involves tailoring medical treatment to the individual characteristics of each patient, including their genetic profile. This approach aims to optimize therapeutic efficacy and minimize adverse effects by considering the genetic differences between individuals.

Applications:

1. **Pharmacogenomics:**

   - Pharmacogenomics studies how genetic variations affect an individual's response to drugs. By understanding these genetic differences, clinicians can select the most effective medications and dosages for each patient.

   - For example, variations in the CYP2C9 and VKORC1 genes can influence the metabolism of warfarin, a common anticoagulant. Genotyping these genes helps determine the appropriate warfarin dose for each patient.

2. **Targeted Therapies:**

   - Personalized medicine includes the development of targeted therapies that specifically address the genetic mutations driving a disease.

   - For example, trastuzumab (Herceptin) is a targeted therapy for breast cancer patients with HER2 gene amplification.

Benefits:

- Improved treatment efficacy by selecting therapies that are more likely to be effective based on genetic information.

- Reduced risk of adverse drug reactions by avoiding medications that a patient may metabolize poorly or be hypersensitive to.

- More efficient healthcare by reducing trial-and-error prescribing and unnecessary treatments.

7.2 Genetic Testing and Screening

Genetic testing involves analyzing DNA to identify changes or mutations that may indicate the presence of a genetic disorder or an increased risk of developing certain conditions. There are several types of genetic tests, each serving a different purpose.

Types of Genetic Testing:

1. **Diagnostic Testing:**

   - Used to confirm or rule out a specific genetic disorder in individuals showing symptoms.

   - For example, diagnostic testing for cystic fibrosis involves detecting mutations in the CFTR gene.

2. **Predictive and Pre-symptomatic Testing:**

   - Used to assess the risk of developing a genetic disorder before symptoms appear.

   - For example, BRCA1 and BRCA2 gene testing can predict the risk of breast and ovarian cancer.

3. **Carrier Testing:**

   - Identifies individuals who carry one copy of a gene mutation that, when present in two copies, causes a genetic disorder.

   - Commonly offered to individuals with a family history of genetic disorders or specific ethnic groups with a higher prevalence of certain conditions.

4. **Prenatal and Newborn Screening:**

- Prenatal screening tests for genetic abnormalities in a fetus, such as Down syndrome.

- Newborn screening detects genetic disorders early in life, allowing for prompt intervention and treatment. For example, newborns are commonly screened for phenylketonuria (PKU).

7.3 Genomic Medicine in Practice

Overview:

Genomic medicine applies the knowledge of the genome to clinical practice, improving the diagnosis, treatment, and prevention of diseases. Several areas of medicine have been transformed by genomic insights.

Applications:

1. **Cancer Genomics:**

   - Cancer genomics involves identifying genetic mutations and alterations in cancer cells to develop targeted therapies.

   - Techniques such as next-generation sequencing (NGS) are used to sequence tumor DNA, revealing mutations that drive cancer progression.

   - Targeted therapies, such as tyrosine kinase inhibitors for chronic myeloid leukemia (e.g., imatinib), are designed to specifically target these mutations.

Case Study:

- The identification of EGFR mutations in non-small cell lung cancer has led to the development of targeted therapies, such as gefitinib and erlotinib, which are effective in patients with these mutations.

2. **Cardiovascular Genomics:**

   - Cardiovascular genomics focuses on understanding the genetic risk factors for heart disease and developing preventive strategies.

- Genetic testing can identify individuals at high risk for conditions such as familial hypercholesterolemia, a genetic disorder that causes high cholesterol levels and increases the risk of heart disease.

- Personalized treatment plans, including lifestyle changes and medications, can be implemented based on genetic risk profiles.

Case Study:

- Genotyping of the PCSK9 gene has led to the development of PCSK9 inhibitors, a new class of drugs that lower cholesterol levels and reduce the risk of cardiovascular events.

3. **Neurogenomics:**

- Neurogenomics investigates the genetic basis of neurological disorders and mental health conditions.

- Genetic testing and research have identified numerous genetic variants associated with disorders such as Alzheimer's disease, Parkinson's disease, and schizophrenia.

- Understanding these genetic factors can lead to early diagnosis, targeted treatments, and the development of new therapeutic approaches.

Case Study:

- Variants in the APOE gene are associated with an increased risk of Alzheimer's disease. Identifying individuals with these variants allows for early interventions and the potential development of preventive treatments.

Chapter 21

Ethical, Legal, and Social Implications of Genomics

8.1 Ethical Considerations

The rapid advancement in genomics raises several ethical issues that need careful consideration to ensure the responsible use of genetic information. These ethical considerations include informed consent, privacy and confidentiality, and the potential for genetic discrimination.

Key Ethical Issues:

1. **Informed Consent for Genetic Testing:**

   - Informed consent is a fundamental ethical principle requiring individuals to be fully aware of the implications, risks, and benefits of genetic testing before undergoing the procedure.

   - Individuals should understand what the test results may reveal, how the information will be used, and who will have access to their genetic data.

   - The process should involve clear communication and should be voluntary, ensuring that individuals are making an informed decision without coercion.

2. **Privacy and Confidentiality of Genetic Information:**

   - Genetic information is highly sensitive and personal. Safeguarding the privacy and confidentiality of genetic data is crucial.

   - Healthcare providers and researchers must implement stringent measures to protect genetic data from unauthorized access, breaches, and misuse.

   - Policies should be in place to determine how genetic information is stored, shared, and used, ensuring that individuals' genetic data is protected throughout their lifetime.

3. **Genetic Discrimination:**

- Genetic discrimination occurs when individuals are treated unfairly based on their genetic information. This can affect employment, insurance coverage, and social interactions.

- Concerns about genetic discrimination may deter individuals from undergoing genetic testing or participating in genomic research.

- Ethical guidelines and legal protections are necessary to prevent genetic discrimination and promote the fair use of genetic information.

8.2 Legal Aspects

The legal landscape of genomics involves regulations and laws designed to protect individuals' genetic information and ensure its ethical use. One of the key legislations in this area is the Genetic Information Nondiscrimination Act (GINA) in the United States.

Key Legal Protections:

1. **Genetic Information Nondiscrimination Act (GINA):**

   - GINA, enacted in 2008, is a federal law in the United States that prohibits genetic discrimination in health insurance and employment.

   - It ensures that individuals cannot be denied health coverage or charged higher premiums based on their genetic information.

   - Employers are prohibited from using genetic information in hiring, firing, job assignments, or promotions.

2. **Other Legal Frameworks:**

   - Various countries have their own legal frameworks to protect genetic information and prevent discrimination.

- o For example, the European Union's General Data Protection Regulation (GDPR) includes provisions for the protection of genetic data as sensitive personal information.

- o Legal frameworks should evolve with advancements in genomics to address emerging ethical and privacy concerns.

8.3 Social Implications

The social implications of genomics are broad and multifaceted, influencing public perception, access to genetic services, and potential disparities in healthcare.

Key Social Implications:

1. **Public Perception and Acceptance:**

   - o The public's understanding and perception of genomic technologies significantly impact their acceptance and utilization.

   - o Education and awareness programs are essential to inform the public about the benefits, limitations, and ethical considerations of genomics.

   - o Misconceptions and fears about genetic testing and genetic information need to be addressed through transparent communication.

2. **Access to Genetic Services:**

   - o Access to genetic testing and services should be equitable, ensuring that all individuals, regardless of socioeconomic status, have the opportunity to benefit from genomic advancements.

   - o Barriers to access, such as cost, lack of healthcare infrastructure, and limited availability of genetic counselors, need to be addressed.

3. **Disparities in Healthcare:**

   - o Genomics has the potential to exacerbate existing disparities in healthcare if not managed inclusively.

- o Efforts should be made to ensure that genomic research includes diverse populations to avoid health disparities.

- o Policies and initiatives should focus on providing equitable access to genomic technologies and personalized medicine.

Chapter 22

Future Directions in Human Genomics

9.1 Emerging Technologies

The field of human genomics is rapidly evolving, driven by the development of new technologies that enhance our ability to understand and manipulate the genome.

Emerging Technologies:

1. **CRISPR and Genome Editing:**

   o **Overview:**

     - CRISPR (Clustered Regularly Interspaced Short Palindromic Repeats) and associated protein Cas9 have revolutionized genome editing, allowing for precise modifications of the DNA.

   o **Mechanism:**

     - The CRISPR-Cas9 system uses a guide RNA to target a specific DNA sequence, where the Cas9 enzyme creates a double-strand break. This break can then be repaired by the cell, allowing for the insertion, deletion, or replacement of DNA sequences.

   o **Applications:**

     - Correction of genetic mutations causing diseases.

     - Creation of genetically modified organisms for research.

     - Potential for gene therapy in treating inherited disorders.

   o **Ethical Considerations:**

- Issues surrounding germline editing, potential off-target effects, and the implications of editing human embryos.

2. **Single-Cell Genomics:**

   o **Overview:**

   - Single-cell genomics involves analyzing the genetic material at the single-cell level, providing insights into cellular diversity and function.

   o **Technologies:**

   - Single-cell RNA sequencing (scRNA-seq) allows for the examination of gene expression profiles in individual cells.

   - Single-cell DNA sequencing enables the study of genetic variations and mutations within individual cells.

   o **Applications:**

   - Understanding cellular heterogeneity in tissues and tumors.

   - Identifying rare cell populations and their roles in development and disease.

   - Insights into stem cell differentiation and immune responses.

3. **Long-Read Sequencing Technologies:**

   o **Overview:**

   - Long-read sequencing technologies, such as those developed by Pacific Biosciences (PacBio) and Oxford Nanopore Technologies, provide longer read lengths compared to traditional short-read sequencing.

   o **Advantages:**

   - Improved genome assembly and resolution of complex genomic regions.

   - Better detection of structural variations, repetitive sequences, and haplotype phasing.

- o **Applications:**

  - Comprehensive characterization of genomes, including large and complex organisms.

  - Identification of genetic variants associated with diseases.

  - Enhancing our understanding of genetic diversity and evolution.

9.2 Genomics and Public Health

Integrating genomics into public health initiatives holds the potential to transform disease prevention, management, and overall health outcomes. Population genomics studies help identify genetic risk factors and inform public health strategies.

Applications:

1. **Disease Prevention:**

   - o Genomic screening programs can identify individuals at risk for genetic disorders, enabling early intervention and preventive measures.

   - o Public health campaigns can be tailored to address the specific genetic susceptibilities of populations.

2. **Epidemiology:**

   - o Genomic data can be used to track the spread of infectious diseases and understand the genetic factors influencing disease susceptibility and resistance.

   - o Genomic epidemiology provides insights into pathogen evolution and outbreak dynamics, aiding in the development of effective control measures.

3. **Precision Public Health:**

   - o Precision public health leverages genomic data to develop targeted interventions and policies that address the health needs of specific populations.

o It aims to reduce health disparities by providing personalized health recommendations based on genetic information.

9.3 The Role of Big Data

The increasing volume of genomic data generated by sequencing technologies and genomic studies necessitates advanced computational tools for analysis and interpretation. Big data analytics, including machine learning and artificial intelligence (AI), are essential for extracting meaningful insights from large genomic datasets.

Applications:

1. **Data Integration and Management:**

   o Effective storage, management, and integration of large genomic datasets from diverse sources are critical for comprehensive analyses.

   o Cloud-based platforms and high-performance computing are employed to handle the vast amount of data generated.

2. **Machine Learning and AI:**

   o Machine learning algorithms can identify patterns and associations in genomic data that are not apparent through traditional analytical methods.

   o AI-driven tools can predict disease risk, identify potential therapeutic targets, and personalize treatment plans based on genetic profiles.

3. **Predictive Modeling:**

   o Predictive models using genomic data can forecast disease outcomes, treatment responses, and epidemiological trends.

   o These models enhance clinical decision-making and public health planning.

Chapter 23

Case Studies in Human Genomics

10.1 Case Study 1: Cancer Genomics

Cancer genomics focuses on understanding the genetic mutations and alterations that drive cancer development. By identifying these driver mutations, researchers can develop targeted therapies tailored to an individual's genetic profile.

Key Points:

1. **Identification of Driver Mutations in Cancer:**

   o Driver mutations are genetic alterations that contribute to cancer progression by conferring a growth advantage to the cells.

   o Techniques such as next-generation sequencing (NGS) are used to identify these mutations in tumor DNA.

2. **Development of Targeted Therapies Based on Genetic Profiles:**

   o Targeted therapies are designed to specifically inhibit the activity of proteins produced by mutated genes.

   o These therapies are more precise and often less toxic than traditional chemotherapy, as they aim at cancer-specific pathways.

3. **Example: The Use of BRCA1/BRCA2 Mutation Testing in Breast and Ovarian Cancer:**

   o Mutations in the BRCA1 and BRCA2 genes significantly increase the risk of breast and ovarian cancer.

   o Genetic testing for BRCA1/BRCA2 mutations helps identify individuals at high risk, allowing for preventive measures such as enhanced screening, prophylactic surgery, or targeted therapies.

- o PARP inhibitors, such as olaparib, are effective in treating cancers with BRCA1/BRCA2 mutations by exploiting the concept of synthetic lethality.

10.2 Case Study 2: Cardiovascular Genomics

Cardiovascular genomics explores the genetic factors underlying cardiovascular diseases. It aims to identify genetic variants associated with inherited cardiovascular conditions and develop preventive strategies based on genomic information.

Key Points:

1. **Genetic Basis of Inherited Cardiovascular Diseases:**

   - o Many cardiovascular diseases, such as hypertrophic cardiomyopathy and familial hypercholesterolemia, have a strong genetic component.

   - o Identifying genetic mutations associated with these diseases can aid in diagnosis, risk assessment, and family screening.

2. **Applications of Genomics in Preventive Cardiology:**

   - o Genomic information can guide personalized preventive measures, such as lifestyle modifications and pharmacological interventions.

   - o Early identification of at-risk individuals allows for timely interventions to prevent disease onset or progression.

3. **Example: Identifying Genetic Variants Associated with Familial Hypercholesterolemia:**

   - o Familial hypercholesterolemia (FH) is an inherited disorder characterized by high cholesterol levels and an increased risk of coronary artery disease.

   - o Mutations in the LDLR, APOB, and PCSK9 genes are commonly associated with FH.

   - o Genetic testing for these variants enables early diagnosis and the implementation of aggressive cholesterol-lowering therapies, such as statins and PCSK9 inhibitors, to reduce cardiovascular risk.

10.3 Case Study 3: Neurogenomics

Neurogenomics focuses on the genetic factors that contribute to neurological and mental health disorders. By studying the genetic basis of these conditions, researchers aim to improve diagnosis, treatment, and understanding of brain function and dysfunction.

Key Points:

1. **Genetic Factors in Neurodegenerative Diseases:**

   o Neurodegenerative diseases, such as Alzheimer's disease, Parkinson's disease, and amyotrophic lateral sclerosis (ALS), often have a genetic component.

   o Identifying genetic mutations associated with these diseases can provide insights into their pathogenesis and potential therapeutic targets.

2. **Genomic Approaches to Understanding Mental Health Disorders:**

   o Mental health disorders, including schizophrenia, bipolar disorder, and major depression, are influenced by a complex interplay of genetic and environmental factors.

   o Genome-wide association studies (GWAS) have identified numerous genetic variants associated with these disorders, shedding light on their biological underpinnings.

3. **Example: The Role of APOE Gene Variants in Alzheimer's Disease:**

   o The APOE gene encodes apolipoprotein E, a protein involved in lipid metabolism.

   o Variants of the APOE gene, particularly the APOE ε4 allele, are associated with an increased risk of developing Alzheimer's disease.

   o Genetic testing for APOE variants can help assess the risk of Alzheimer's disease and inform clinical decisions, such as early interventions and participation in clinical trials.

Ayurgenomics: Integrating Ayurveda and Genomics

Ayurgenomics:

Ayurgenomics aims to bridge the gap between traditional Ayurvedic concepts and modern genomic science. By studying the genetic basis of Prakriti, researchers hope to uncover the molecular mechanisms underlying the dosha-related traits and health tendencies.

Key Concepts:

1. **Genetic Markers and Prakriti:**

   o Research has identified specific genetic markers associated with different Prakriti types. For example, polymorphisms in genes related to metabolism, immune function, and neural processes have been linked to Vata, Pitta, and Kapha constitutions.

2. **Gene Expression and Doshas:**

   o Studies have shown that the expression levels of certain genes vary among individuals with different Prakriti types. These variations can influence physiological functions, disease susceptibility, and response to treatments.

3. **Epigenetics and Prakriti:**

   o Epigenetic modifications, such as DNA methylation and histone modification, can affect gene expression without altering the underlying DNA sequence. Environmental factors, lifestyle, and diet, which are central to Ayurvedic practices, can induce epigenetic changes that impact Prakriti.

The Practical Applications of Ayurgenomics

Personalized Medicine:

1. **Tailored Health Recommendations:**

   o Understanding an individual's Prakriti and genetic makeup allows for personalized health recommendations. Ayurvedic practitioners can suggest specific diets, lifestyle changes, and herbal treatments tailored to the individual's constitution.

2. **Disease Prevention and Management:**

   o Identifying genetic predispositions linked to Prakriti can help in early detection and prevention of diseases. For instance, individuals with a Pitta constitution and genetic markers for inflammatory conditions can adopt preventive measures to reduce their risk.

3. **Optimized Treatment Strategies:**

   o Ayurgenomics can guide the selection of the most effective treatments based on an individual's genetic profile and Prakriti. This approach enhances the efficacy of Ayurvedic therapies and minimizes adverse effects.

The Interplay Between Prakriti and Genetics

Below is a conceptual diagram illustrating the relationship between Prakriti, genetic markers, gene expression, and personalized medicine.

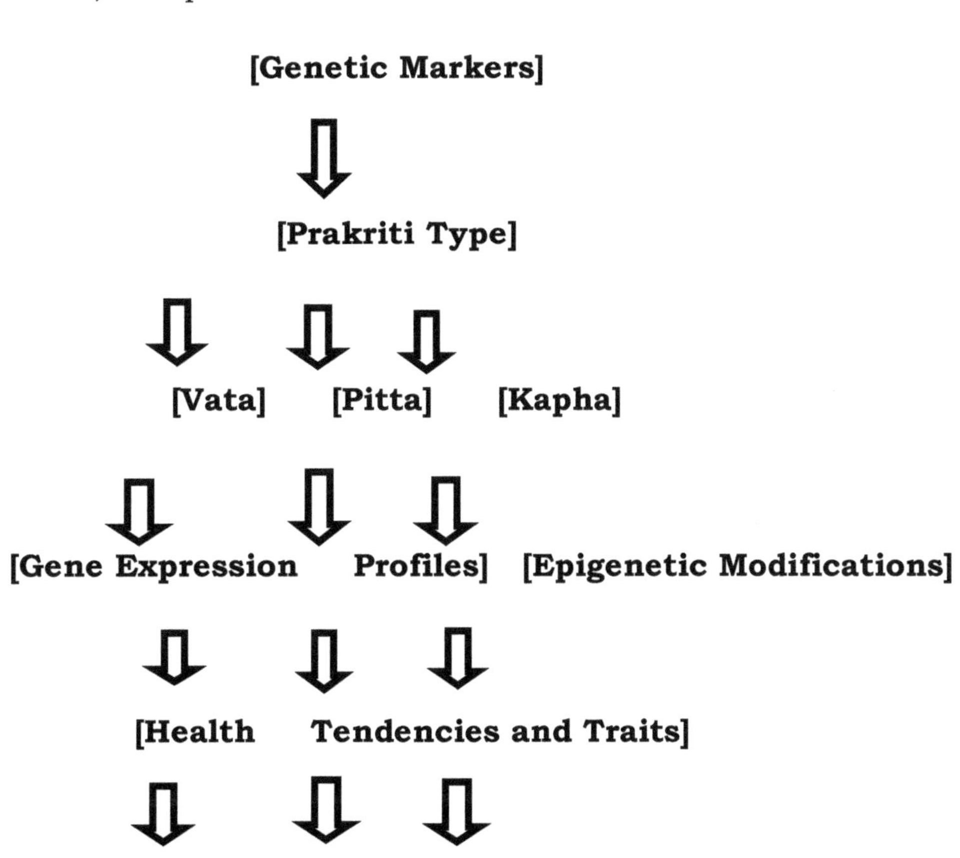

[Personalized   Health Recommendations]

Ayurgenomics offers a promising avenue for integrating the wisdom of Ayurveda with the precision of modern genomics. By exploring the genetic basis of Prakriti, researchers can enhance our understanding of individual health profiles and develop personalized approaches to disease prevention and treatment. This integration not only validates the ancient Ayurvedic principles but also paves the way for a more holistic and effective healthcare system.

Chapter -24

Role of Prakriti in Ayurgenomics

Prakriti, a core concept in *Ayurveda,* represents the unique constitution or nature of an individual. It is believed to govern various aspects of health, disease susceptibility, mental traits, and physical characteristics. In Ayurgenomics, the concept of *Prakriti* plays a pivotal role in integrating ancient Ayurvedic principles with modern genomic science. Understanding how *Prakriti* influences gene expression, metabolic pathways, and disease susceptibility helps to tailor personalized healthcare based on an individual's genetic makeup.

This section explores the detailed role of *Prakriti* in Ayurgenomics, with an emphasis on how it bridges the gap between traditional medicine and modern genomics.

1. Genomic Correlates of *Prakriti*:

In Ayurgenomics, the concept of *Prakriti* is explored through the lens of genomics. Studies have found that individuals of different *Prakriti* types exhibit distinct genetic markers and molecular pathways, which correspond to their physiological traits and disease predispositions. The mapping of these markers to modern genomic data provides a scientific framework for personalized medicine.

For example:

- *Vata Prakriti* individuals tend to have genes related to neurotransmitter regulation, correlating with their traits of mental agility, creativity, and quick response to stimuli.

- *Pitta Prakriti* individuals may have genes associated with metabolism, inflammation, and immune response, explaining their strong digestion, sharp intellect, and predisposition to inflammatory conditions.

- *Kapha Prakriti* individuals often exhibit genetic markers linked to anabolic processes and slower metabolism, which aligns with their physical endurance, calm nature, and tendency to gain weight.

2. Role of *Prakriti* in Disease Susceptibility:

In Ayurgenomics, *Prakriti* is considered a critical factor in determining an individual's susceptibility to diseases. Each *Prakriti* type is believed to have a predisposition to specific conditions, and genomic research supports this claim by identifying genetic variants linked to these conditions.

For instance:

- **Vata Prakriti**: Individuals with *Vata* dominance are prone to neurological and psychiatric disorders such as anxiety, insomnia, and degenerative diseases. Genomic studies suggest that variations in neurotransmitter-related genes (e.g., dopamine receptors) may contribute to these traits.

- **Pitta Prakriti**: People with a *Pitta* constitution are more susceptible to inflammatory disorders such as skin diseases, acid reflux, and cardiovascular problems. Genomic markers related to pro-inflammatory cytokines and metabolism have been found to be more prevalent in these individuals.

- **Kapha Prakriti**: Individuals with *Kapha* dominance are more likely to suffer from conditions related to obesity, diabetes, and respiratory problems. Genes associated with lipid metabolism and insulin resistance are often linked to these predispositions in *Kapha* individuals.

3. *Prakriti* and Epigenetics:

Epigenetics is the study of how environmental factors such as diet, lifestyle, and stress can influence gene expression without changing the underlying DNA sequence. In Ayurgenomics, *Prakriti* is thought to influence not only genetic predispositions but also epigenetic modifications that can either protect against or increase the risk of certain diseases.

For example:

- A person with a *Pitta Prakriti* who follows a lifestyle conducive to reducing inflammation (cooling foods, stress management) may be able to mitigate the genetic predisposition for inflammatory disorders.

- Conversely, a *Kapha Prakriti* individual who leads a sedentary lifestyle and consumes heavy, sweet foods may exacerbate their genetic predisposition to obesity and diabetes through negative epigenetic changes.

By understanding both the genomic and epigenetic factors associated with *Prakriti*, Ayurgenomics aims to offer a more comprehensive approach to health management and disease prevention.

4. Personalized Medicine and *Prakriti*:

The concept of *Prakriti* provides a framework for personalized medicine in Ayurgenomics. Since each *Prakriti* type has unique physiological and psychological characteristics, treatment plans can be tailored to the individual's constitution, ensuring better outcomes. Personalized medicine in Ayurgenomics focuses on the following aspects:

1. **Drug Metabolism**: Different *Prakriti* types respond differently to medications. For instance, *Vata Prakriti* individuals may metabolize drugs related to neurotransmission more rapidly, requiring specific dosages and formulations. Genomic analysis of drug-metabolizing enzymes (like cytochrome P450) helps optimize treatments based on *Prakriti*.

2. **Diet and Lifestyle**: Each *Prakriti* has distinct dietary and lifestyle needs. Ayurgenomics uses genetic information to refine these recommendations, helping individuals make choices that align with their constitution and genomic predispositions.

3. **Preventive Healthcare**: By recognizing genetic predispositions based on *Prakriti*, Ayurgenomics enables preventive interventions tailored to each individual. For example, *Kapha Prakriti* individuals may benefit from early interventions to manage weight, while *Pitta Prakriti* individuals can take steps to reduce inflammation.

5. Research Evidence Supporting *Prakriti* in Genomics:

Several research studies have provided evidence for the correlation between *Prakriti* and genomic variations. These studies show that genetic polymorphisms in specific genes can predict *Prakriti* types, supporting the Ayurvedic view that individuals with different constitutions exhibit distinct biological traits.

Examples include:

- **CYP2C19** Gene: This gene, responsible for metabolizing many drugs, has been studied in relation to *Prakriti*. Variants of this gene have been found to differ significantly between *Vata, Pitta*, and *Kapha* individuals, influencing drug response.

- **HLA (Human Leukocyte Antigen)** Genes: These genes, which are involved in immune system regulation, show distinct patterns in individuals with different *Prakriti*. For instance, *Pitta Prakriti* individuals may show a higher expression of certain inflammatory markers.

- **Oxidative Stress and Antioxidant Genes**: Individuals with *Kapha Prakriti* tend to have higher antioxidant capacity, while those with *Pitta Prakriti* may exhibit greater oxidative stress markers, influencing their susceptibility to conditions like cardiovascular diseases.

6. *Prakriti* and the Future of Genomics:

In the future, Ayurgenomics aims to refine the understanding of *Prakriti* by incorporating more advanced genomic and molecular biology tools. Whole genome sequencing, transcriptomics, and metabolomics can be used to further dissect the molecular signatures associated with different *Prakriti* types. This could lead to:

- **Precision Medicine**: Combining *Prakriti* with genomic data allows for precise, individualized treatment plans. For instance, therapies for metabolic disorders could be tailored based on the interaction between *Prakriti* and genetic predisposition.

- **Nutrigenomics**: The study of how diet interacts with genes based on *Prakriti* will be a focus in the future. This will allow more accurate dietary guidelines to be developed, preventing diseases and improving health outcomes.

Chapter -25

Genomics in Modern Healthcare Systems

Introduction: Genomics is the study of the entire genome of an organism, including its structure, function, evolution, and interaction with the environment. In modern healthcare systems, genomics has revolutionized the way diseases are understood, diagnosed, treated, and prevented. The integration of genomics into healthcare enables personalized or precision medicine, where treatment and prevention strategies are tailored to an individual's genetic makeup. This approach is transforming traditional medicine by providing more accurate diagnoses, predicting disease risks, and optimizing therapies based on genetic profiles.

This section explores the various ways genomics is being applied in modern healthcare systems and the potential benefits and challenges associated with its use.

1. Role of Genomics in Disease Diagnosis:

Genomic technologies have significantly improved the accuracy of disease diagnosis, particularly for genetic and hereditary conditions. Techniques such as Whole Genome Sequencing (WGS), Whole Exome Sequencing (WES), and genome-wide association studies (GWAS) help identify genetic mutations or variations that may be responsible for diseases.

- **Rare Genetic Disorders:** Genomic sequencing allows clinicians to identify rare genetic mutations that cause inherited diseases. This can lead to earlier and more precise diagnoses, reducing the diagnostic odyssey for patients with conditions such as cystic fibrosis, Duchenne muscular dystrophy, and Huntington's disease.

- **Cancer Genomics:** Genomics plays a vital role in understanding the genetic mutations driving different types of cancer. Tumor sequencing allows for the identification of specific mutations, enabling oncologists to tailor treatment strategies based on the genetic profile of the tumor (e.g., targeted therapies for mutations in the *EGFR*, *BRCA1/2*, or *KRAS* genes).

- **Infectious Disease Genomics:** Genomics has also enhanced the diagnosis and tracking of infectious diseases. Pathogen sequencing helps in identifying drug-resistant strains of bacteria or viruses, guiding more effective treatment strategies (e.g., sequencing of *SARS-CoV-2* variants during the COVID-19 pandemic).

2. Genomics and Personalized Medicine:

Personalized or precision medicine tailors medical care to individual patients based on their genetic makeup, lifestyle, and environmental factors. Genomics has made personalized medicine a reality in many areas of healthcare, allowing for treatments to be more effective and minimizing adverse reactions.

- **Pharmacogenomics:** This branch of genomics studies how an individual's genetic makeup affects their response to drugs. By understanding genetic variations in drug-metabolizing enzymes (such as *CYP450*), clinicians can predict how patients will respond to certain medications. This reduces the risk of adverse drug reactions and increases the efficacy of treatments. For instance, genetic testing for variations in the *CYP2C9* and *VKORC1* genes helps determine optimal dosing of warfarin, a commonly used blood thinner.

- **Targeted Cancer Therapies:** In oncology, genomics has led to the development of targeted therapies that specifically attack cancer cells with certain genetic mutations. For example, drugs like trastuzumab (Herceptin) target HER2-positive breast cancer, while imatinib (Gleevec) targets the *BCR-ABL* fusion gene in chronic myeloid leukemia (CML).

- **Gene Therapy:** Genomic research has paved the way for gene therapies, which aim to treat or even cure genetic disorders by correcting defective genes. For example, *Luxturna* is a gene therapy approved for treating inherited retinal diseases caused by mutations in the *RPE65* gene.

3. Genomics in Preventive Healthcare:

Genomics is also transforming preventive healthcare by enabling risk prediction for common complex diseases such as heart disease, diabetes, and cancer. By analyzing an individual's genetic predispositions, healthcare providers can offer personalized prevention plans, including lifestyle modifications, regular screenings, and early interventions.

- **Polygenic Risk Scores (PRS):** These scores are calculated based on the cumulative effect of multiple genetic variants associated with a disease. For example, a high PRS for cardiovascular disease could prompt earlier monitoring and lifestyle interventions, potentially preventing heart attacks or strokes.

- **Newborn Screening:** Genomic technologies are being incorporated into newborn screening programs to detect genetic conditions early in life, such as phenylketonuria (PKU) and spinal muscular atrophy (SMA). Early detection allows for timely interventions that can prevent severe complications or even death.

4. Reproductive Genomics:

Genomics has a significant impact on reproductive health, helping couples make informed decisions about family planning and offering insights into genetic disorders that may affect their offspring.

- **Preconception Genetic Testing:** Couples can undergo genetic testing to assess their risk of passing on hereditary conditions to their children, such as cystic fibrosis or sickle cell disease. This information helps in making informed reproductive choices.

- **Prenatal Genetic Testing:** Non-invasive prenatal testing (NIPT) allows for early detection of chromosomal abnormalities like Down syndrome by analyzing fetal DNA circulating in the mother's blood. This test is safer than invasive methods such as amniocentesis.

- **Assisted Reproductive Technologies (ART):** Genomics is increasingly being integrated into ART, such as in-vitro fertilization (IVF), through techniques like preimplantation genetic diagnosis (PGD). PGD screens embryos for genetic abnormalities before implantation, improving the chances of a successful pregnancy and reducing the risk of genetic disorders.

5. Genomics in Infectious Disease Control:

Genomics plays a critical role in understanding and controlling infectious diseases. Pathogen genomics allows scientists to track the spread of diseases, identify mutations, and develop targeted treatments or vaccines.

- **Epidemiological Surveillance:** Genome sequencing of pathogens, such as bacteria, viruses, and fungi, provides insights into transmission patterns and helps in tracking outbreaks. This was crucial during the COVID-19 pandemic, where genomic surveillance of SARS-CoV-2 helped identify emerging variants and inform public health measures.

- **Antimicrobial Resistance (AMR):** Genomic tools help in identifying genetic mutations that confer drug resistance in pathogens. This allows clinicians to choose the most effective antibiotics and helps in the development of new treatments to combat AMR.

6. Ethical Considerations in Genomics:

The integration of genomics into healthcare comes with several ethical considerations that need to be addressed to ensure responsible use.

- **Privacy and Data Security:** Genomic data is highly personal and sensitive. There is a risk of genetic information being misused by insurers or employers. Ensuring the confidentiality and security of genomic data is paramount in modern healthcare systems.

- **Informed Consent:** Patients undergoing genomic testing need to provide informed consent, understanding the potential outcomes of the tests, including incidental findings that may reveal unknown genetic risks for unrelated conditions.

- **Equitable Access:** As genomics-based healthcare becomes more widespread, there is a risk of creating disparities in access to these advanced technologies. Ensuring equitable access to genomic testing and personalized treatments is a key challenge for healthcare systems.

7. Challenges of Integrating Genomics into Healthcare:

While genomics has the potential to transform healthcare, there are several challenges that must be overcome for its full integration into clinical practice.

- **Cost and Accessibility:** Although the cost of genomic sequencing has decreased significantly, it is still relatively expensive and may not be accessible to all populations. Efforts are needed to make genomic testing more affordable and widely available.

- **Complexity of Data Interpretation:** Genomic data is complex and requires specialized knowledge to interpret. Healthcare providers need to be trained in genomics to apply this information effectively in patient care.

- **Integration with Electronic Health Records (EHRs):** Incorporating genomic data into EHRs in a way that is easily accessible and interpretable for clinicians is a major challenge. Healthcare systems need to develop infrastructure to manage and utilize large-scale genomic data efficiently.

8. Future Directions of Genomics in Healthcare:

The future of genomics in healthcare looks promising, with several exciting advancements on the horizon.

- **CRISPR and Gene Editing:** The development of CRISPR-Cas9 technology has revolutionized the field of gene editing, allowing precise modifications to DNA. This technology holds the potential to treat genetic disorders by directly correcting faulty genes.

- **Pharmacogenomics Expansion:** As more genomic data becomes available, pharmacogenomics will expand to include a broader range of drugs and conditions, enabling more personalized drug therapies for common diseases such as hypertension, diabetes, and mental health disorders.

- **Artificial Intelligence and Genomics:** AI and machine learning tools are being developed to analyze large genomic datasets, uncovering new insights into disease mechanisms and aiding in drug discovery. AI could also help in interpreting complex genomic data for clinical decision-making.

REFERENCES

1. Aggarwal, A., Arora, S., & Chandersekhar, C. N. (2010). Genetic Basis of Ayurvedic Types of Constitution (Prakriti). Indian Journal of Human Genetics, 16(1), 51–56.

2. Rotti, H., Raval, R., Anchan, S., Kanchan, K., Bellampalli, R., & Bhavana, K. (2014). Determinants of Prakriti, the human constitution types of Indian traditional medicine and its correlation with contemporary science. Journal of Ayurveda and Integrative Medicine, 5(3), 167–175.

3. Prasher, B., Negi, S., Aggarwal, S., Mandal, A. K., Sethi, T. P., & Deshmukh, S. R. (2008). Whole genome expression and biochemical correlates of extreme constitutional types defined in Ayurveda. Journal of Translational Medicine, 6, 48.

4. Chaudhary, A., & Singh, N. (2010). Contribution of World Health Organization in the global acceptance of Ayurveda. Journal of Ayurveda and Integrative Medicine, 1(2), 81–85.

5. Patwardhan, B., Warude, D., Pushpangadan, P., & Bhatt, N. (2005). Ayurveda and traditional Chinese medicine: A comparative overview. Evidence-Based Complementary and Alternative Medicine, 2(4), 465–473.

6. Hankey, A. (2005). The scientific value of Ayurveda. Journal of Alternative and Complementary Medicine, 11(2), 221–225.

7. Patwardhan, B. (2014). The quest for evidence-based Ayurveda: Lessons learned. Current Science, 107(9), 1550–1556.

8. Mishra, A., Shukla, S., & Sundar, S. (2011). Development of ayurgenomics: An integration of Ayurveda and genomics for personalized medicine. Indian Journal of Traditional Knowledge, 10(4), 589–593.

9. Prasher, B., Varma, B., & Kumar, A. (2017). Ayurgenomics for stratified medicine: Current state and future perspectives. Scientific Reports, 7, 15786.

10. Bhavana, K., Rotti, H., & Prasher, B. (2011). Exploring the scientific basis of Prakriti: Correlation of genomic diversity with Prakriti types. International Journal of Ayurveda Research, 2(1), 50–54.

11. Frawley, D. (1997). Ayurveda and the Mind: The Healing of Consciousness. Lotus

Press.

12. Lad, V. (2002). Textbook of Ayurveda: Fundamental Principles. Ayurvedic Press.

13. Sharma, P. V. (1996). Classical Uses of Medicinal Plants. Chaukhambha Visvabharati.

14. Bhagwan Dash, V. (1985). Fundamentals of Ayurvedic Medicine. Concept Publishing Company.

15. Sharma, H., & Clark, C. (1998). Contemporary Ayurveda: Medicine and Research in Maharishi Ayur-Veda. Churchill Livingstone.

16. Deepak, K. K., & Prasher, B. (2012). Concepts of human physiology in Ayurveda: Exploring the scientific basis. Current Science, 102(10), 1406–1414.

17. Tripathi, Y. B., & Singh, R. H. (2010). The basic tenets of ayurvedic pharmacology and their applications in pharmaceutical research. Journal of Ayurveda and Integrative Medicine, 1(4), 244–248.

18. Tripathi, J. S., & Tiwari, S. K. (2008). Integrative approach of genomics and Ayurveda for personalized medicine. AYU, 29(1), 32–38.

19. Singh, R. H. (2003). Exploring issues in the development of Ayurvedic research methodology. Journal of Ayurveda, 2(1), 3–10.

20. Patwardhan, B., & Mashelkar, R. A. (2009). Traditional medicine-inspired approaches to drug discovery: Can Ayurveda show the way forward? Drug Discovery Today, 14(15-16), 804–811.